LETTERS TO MAMA

Anita Ogbonna

LETTERS TO MAMA

ANITA OGBONNA

Anita Ogbonna

Copyright ©2016 Anita Ogbonna

ISBN: 978-978-54741-1-4

All rights reserved.
No part of this book may be reproduced, distributed, stored in a retrieval system or transmitted, in any form or by any means, electronic, electrostatic, magnetic tape, mechanical, photocopying, recording or otherwise without prior written permission from the Publisher.
For information about permission to reproduce selections from this book, write to info@wrr.ng
National Library of Nigeria Cataloguing-in-Publication Data

Printed and Published in Nigeria by:
Words Rhymes & Rhythm Limited
Suite C309, Global Plaza Plot 366, Obafemi Awolowo Way, Jabi District, Abuja, Nigeria.
08169027757, 08060109295
www.wrr.ng

Letters to Mama

ACKNOWLEDGEMENT

With all sincerity, I want to thank everyone who inspired me while writing this book.

To the Supreme Being who made this possible by granting me courage, wisdom and determination to explore, and for the gift of "creative writing", I will forever be grateful to you for seeing me through this project.

To my beautiful family and my Mother; Mrs.Ogechi Ogbonna. Thank you for being my greatest inspiration. I love you mama.

To my siblings who nicknamed me "petition writer." Thank you.

I thank Shoola Oyindamola and Kanyinsola Olorunnisola of *Sprinng Literary Movement* for taking out time to read the manuscripts of this book like it were theirs.

My profound appreciation also goes to Mr. C. J. Njoku of ReadRight Consulting Services for editing the manuscripts of this book and for the constructive criticism.

My gratitude goes to my friends. Thank you for inspiring me to write. To Pascal Amanfo, you never stopped asking me to write, to my friends, Kelechi, Boma, Maggie, Ebere, Osayi, Tini, Samuel, Racheal and Promise Beshel who is a self-accomplished writer. I appreciate you all for your support.

CONTENTS

ACKNOWLEDGEMENT	- 4 -
COMMENTS	- 7 -
LOVE IS NOT DEFINED BY CIRCUMSTANCES	- 12 -
THE BIRTH	- 13 -
DESTINY OR LUCK?	- 14 -
Dear Mama	- 15 -
THE RIDE	- 16 -
SELF ACCEPTANCE	- 17 -
WISDOM	- 18 -
PEACE WITHIN	- 19 -
A POEM FOR MAMA	- 20 -
UP FOR THE UNKNOWN	- 21 -
SINS AND SECRETS	- 22 -
GOOD PAIN BAD PAIN	- 23 -
SELF WORTH	- 24 -
DECISIONS	- 25 -
VAIN AND UNCERTAIN	- 27 -
WET COALS AND EAST	- 28 -
SOCIALIZE	- 29 -
POIGNANT AND RESTLESS	- 30 -
COVERING SHAME	- 31 -

GOD'S MYSTERY	- 32 -
UNSPOKEN WORDS AND PAIN	- 33 -
A FRUITFUL END IS INNEVITABLE	- 34 -
FRIENDSHIP	- 35 -
IN WEAKNESS, FIND STRENGTH AND BE STRENGTH!	- 36 -
TREASURES	- 37 -
TAKING CHANCES	- 38 -
HOLDING UNTO DEATH FOR LIFE	- 39 -
SELF APPRAISAL	- 40 -
DEAR PILOT, TIME FLIES	- 41 -
STRONG	- 42 -
NAMES AND IDENTITY	- 43 -
HEY MAMA	- 44 -
SOJOURN	- 45 -
NEVER DO MORE THAN YOU WILL BE APPRECIATED FOR	- 46 -
MAMA'S PRAYER	- 47 -
TO ALL THE WORDS THAT MY INK CAN'T TRACE OUT OF MYSELF	- 48 -
SELF DISCOVERY	- 49 -
VICTORY	- 50 -
GRATITUDE	- 51 -
THE END	- 53 -

Anita Ogbonna

COMMENTS

This book is a unique dedication to youthfulness. It is a piece that cuts through the feelings, pains and pleasures of growing. It presents the important relationship between a listening mother and a telling child in a way that encourages love, trust and obedience. I recommend this chef d'oeuvre to all mothers, children, and readers out there.
- *Shoola Oyindamola*
  Author of HEARTBEAT

'Letters to Ma' is a series of intimate conversations that leave footprints on the reader's mind. Though at risk of being described as 'girly', this book is a good read for young and old, male or female.
- *Kukogho Iruesiri Samson*
  CEO WRR Publishers, author of WHAT CAN WORDS DO and I SAID THESE WORDS

Letters to Mama is beautiful and organized book chronicling the journey of a young girl to self-actualization. It projects into the reader at each point the intimacy and bond every daughter should share with her mother.I really like the down to earth way Anita took her imperfections, shortcomings and owned them leaving room for change too. That indeed takes courage. Poems like 'the birth and 'Names and Identity' made me smile. In one sentence, 'Profound'.
- *Oyinkansola Awolo*
  For: OYINKANSVIEW.WORDPRESS.COM

Letters to Mama

I love the different pattern laid down to hold the Interest of the reader, the flexibility gives way for an undefined art which is truly rare and beautiful. It leaves the reader asking for more and more comes in meditation. Also, it depicts an African child penning down conversations that ordinarily won't have happened with the African Mother. I would say it's a must read for mothers who is willing to know their daughters in and out.
- *Rachael Charles*
    Spoken Word Artist

'*LETTERS TO MAMA*' is a uniquely written prose with a style of its own. It is a writing that talks of a perfect relationship between a listening mother and a talking girl. Anita relates the *everyday* activity of a growing woman and paints a clear picture of the challenges faced by such a woman. The book is highly recommended to everyone who wants to know what is going on in the mind of a youth, especially parents.
- *Njoku, C. Justin*
    Chief Consultant, ReadRight Consulting Services

Anita Ogbonna

…let me create and be filled with salt because the world needs that flavor…

Letters to Mama

Dear daughter,

I received your letter. I have been smiling in admiration since I began to read your letter. I am happy you learnt. Some things are better understood when you participate. I am happy with the path you thread.

Baby, don't beat yourself too hard, I know the feel of despair conceded in your words. I have been expecting to read from you because I know you'd soon write, your pen has always been your friend. I am certain by now, you don't think all humans are either the same or can be same, or even share similar views. You were born different and the event at your birth told it all. I wish I'd realized it before this day. As a child, you looked most feeble yet you had a strong will and strength I hope this strength that you have will only bail you from troubles and neither to nor you into them. I often have warned you about the challenges of life they are best kept on the shoulders, not on the head. The head can only carry so much, before aching too badly, and put your neck at risk, with every attempt to empty the weight. Yet for the shoulders, you can only lower your shoulders and let the weight fall when they begin to inconvenience.

I have waited out my eyes to see you feed, though I know you are choosy with food. Yet I have trusted your choices all this years.

When you find the rough looking man with many tongues that bamboozle, be polite and ask him to expatiate. ASAM Tidy the walls alright whilst drying the coal, so you can make indelible prints on the chalk board. You will need to be patient while darkening the board, bearing the smears and brimming with focus.

Anita Ogbonna

Remember the writings and sharper, when the board is darker.
   But Agbarasa stainless always remember: don't do more than you will be appreciated for.

I want to read from you again. I am sure this time, I will be getting all the juicy details. Lest I forget, I advise that you be concise, you'll be happier, if you stop assuming that someone will assume right on your behalf.

Love from your mum,

Mama.

LOVE IS NOT DEFINED BY CIRCUMSTANCES

It was a cold harmattan morning, mama quickly bathed me in the protected presence of the bare skies of my grandfather's compound, I sneezed. Mama shivered spontaneously like a helpless leaf dancing to the thick gust of the peculiar morning. She started singing praises to distract me from the catastrophe that led me to bathing in the cold atmosphere, away from what we used to know as home.

"Nwa oma m, onye naege chukwu nti na eribere ya isi, onye na eteta na ayasina eji otubo ya na egwu –
  egwu, onye na eje eje naayasi na atughi ujo   –   "My dear child, the one who listens and obeys God. The one who wakes in the night to fondle with her belly button, the one who walks bravely in the dark…"

When she poured the last bowl of water on my legs, she told me to start rubbing my palms against each other very fast. *"That is what will make you warm and smart when you go to school."* she teased.

She wanted to rub her palms too, and to show me how to rub mine but she hesitated. Her palms paused, put together like a silent prayer denying the scars from papa's punches and faint scratches of pleasures that mocked her seeming weakness.

Anita Ogbonna

THE BIRTH

The room was charged
with heightened expectations of a successful one –
an eventual smooth delivery.
From inside where I curled up
arrogantly grinning from cheek to cheek
as the air of importance demanded
pushing mama across and beyond
those thin lines of thick pain
I heard the most beautiful words;

She pushed and sweated
until I was out with a shrill cry.
This world with the pleasure I earned
from mama's pain is of what kind?

And so I relished the content
of the weightiness of her beauty
the warmth of my pram and the shine of my clothes.
Soon I started several fights on different nights
for my space between mama and papa.
I couldn't care less how the man fared.
Unpleasant, as much as it was
Mama's hope never left papa's eyes
and he often had his way – not once, not twice
but more times than I could count.

Months passed on and weaning beckoned.
I continued to wonder:
this world in its wickedness,
exhumed by mama's pleasure
is of what kind?

DESTINY OR LUCK?

Little wonder mama filled
the sockets of Papa's eyes
wherever he went.

By sunrise, I had taken a name to call mine
Mama's own was Hope,
Mine, now Grace.
My dusk was done
and I set outwards to dawn.

I see how far I have come
and I wonder if it's luck or destiny

I still wonder:
this world is of what kind?

Anita Ogbonna

4:42pm, 1ˢᵗ June

DEAR MAMA,

It is your little girl, now a lady.

Thank you for teaching me how to rub my palms against each other when I feel cold and how to stand up for others. Life has taught me that that it is what defines a strong woman! Mama, in my lady-ness I am that woman now!

Thank you for teaching me to walk through the streets with an address, to keep the landmark of my destination in mind, and to know a close when I walk into one.

Your little girl is out on the street and she has become a hustler. I just jumped on a bus and just like life, it will go through a couple of streets, but it will get me to my destination eventually.

I love you Mama.

Letters to Mama

3:15pm, 2nd June

THE RIDE

Dear Mama,

It has been quite an interesting ride so far. There are many people with me on this journey, from diverse races, traces, and ethnic groups. Some are quick to love me, and some show no kinder judgement towards me; they would pass for a reservoir of criticism and toxic opinions.

Sometimes, I pick a thing or two from their words and actions, but it has been a tough experience on the streets. I also met some cool people who understand my weird and abstract lifestyle. They jokingly point at my nasty attitudes and habits, the exact ones you always complained about – my mean and stuck up, never-smiley-face, and my oft thoughts about everyone having the same capacity to understand that I am bossy, and my making sarcastic comments like I am void of mistakes myself.

And guess what *(in excitement)* I feel elated working to improve my attitude. I guess the bad habits have cost me more fortunes than I have got. Thank you for teaching me.

I need to run now, the driver is honking that unfriendly horn again. I will write to you soon. I love you Mummy.

Anita Ogbonna

3:15pm, 3rd June

SELF ACCEPTANCE

Dear Mama,

I was going to say this to you, that I have accepted fate. When I opened my palm, I smiled, and the round ball of pride, anger, and pain dropped!

I have cute palms just like yours. They are really soft, the lines are really smooth, and I cannot believe I threw away all those years when I should have admired the beauty in and of my palms. *(Smiles)* I am happy. *(Wipes the tears that drops on her face)*

Mummy, your little girl is happy. I will write to you again and soon. I love you Mummy.

Letters to Mama

2:18pm, 4th June

WISDOM

Dear Mama,

 I miss home. What I miss the most is the folk tales by moonlight. My favorite is this story your daddy once told us about the lion and the tortoise.

 "In the deep forests, there was famine and the lion who was the king of the animals needed to satisfy his hunger and he hoped that a prey would walk into his den. So he sent the town crier to tell all the animals that he was sick and all the animals were to come pay homage to his highness.

 One after another these animals visited the lion in his den. When the tortoise came to the entrance of the lion's den, the lion roared and said, "Mbeezigboenyim. Tortoise my good friend, come in and say hello to me." Then the tortoise in his wisdom said, "how come I can see footprints of a lot of animals who have come in?"

 The lion replied, "Oh yes! Almost all the animals have come to see me." The tortoise then replied, "why are there no footprints of the same animals walking out?"

 Having said that, the tortoise walked away and was the only animal alive"

 Mummy, I didn't trash the caution you packed in my bag. *(Winks).*

Anita Ogbonna

3:14pm, 5th June

PEACE WITHIN

Dear Mama,

Yea! I am super excited because of the lessons I have learnt. I learnt that I am the ocean. I am the ocean! People have taken away from me but I have not run dry, instead I flow. I cut through good and bad, I flow. I was used for good and evil, but mummy I flow.

I have roared and people ran. My strength was too much, and all I did was destroy. I gathered then destroyed. Mummy it took me time to understand that the ocean does not sit in dirt – it flushes them out towards the shore.

I have realized my power. I need to learn how to use it. *(Lets out a sigh of relief).*

The ocean went calm, the ocean carried humans in peace, and she became a serene place where people come to seek rest.

I have found peace within.

A POEM FOR MAMA

Dear mother of an ocean
Leader of a battalion,
Fierce lioness with the gentility of a dove
The specie that assist God in procreation
The fertile soil from which I sprout
I only exhale positively now…

I love you Mummy.

Anita Ogbonna

6:29pm, 7*th* June

UP FOR THE UNKNOWN

Dear Mother,

Today people stopped by the ocean. Great men did fold their pants to pay homage, mortals came to be refreshed.

I cleaned the dirt off the feet of many souls and they were refreshed. Mummy, the once corrosive salt has become flavored salt – it is a necessity, as life tastes better because of it. I am really glad that I stopped by this close.

I am seated on the bus again. My seat belt is fastened. I don't know where my next destination will be – a close, a street or a community? All I know is the address from where I took off.

My destination is uncertain. Regardless of this, I am ready for whatever comes now. I think I sight a rock mummy! It has the waves bridged. I will bath this rock even with its might.

I can see the smiles on your face. *(Stares out the window and smiles)*

I love you Mummy.

Letters to Mama

5:01am, 8th June

SINS AND SECRETS

I didn't tell my sins and secrets yet
It was a prayer point for a brighter day

I didn't tell my worries
Your deep connection let you pet me

I was confused in a city of perfection
Double minded in a street called rejection
But your prayerful life set me aright
Far apart from the shackles of sinful freight

Can I pen down the different words you whispered
"that guy will dump you" confidently uttered.

My baby, my friend
I write countless nothings
To see you smile.
Am willing to bend over
To see you laugh
I will surely cover
My self-esteem to breed higher

Anita Ogbonna

5:11am, 8th June

GOOD PAIN BAD PAIN

Dear Mama,

I bumped into the rock, it is a hard rock. I slammed into it, I the ocean was shattered then calm. I was bruised. *(Takes a deep breath and looks at the time).*

The pace of the rock, static as the past finally soothes me now that I have known it.

This rock has become a shield from the twirling gust of the wind.

SELF WORTH

11:13am, 9th June

Mama,

 I found a diamond. Unlike the rock I bumped into, it does not need waves of water to be renewed. It needs fire to refine it.

 Somewhere on the surface of this earth, a diamond is being drawn, but they would not know its value. They would trash it in the oceans and I will wash it thoroughly. I will polish and refine it. I will beautify it at my banks even though I am not fire.

 There are no more debris lingering around. It has been a long ride, and I am feeling sleepy. *(The car makes a halt, then navigates into another street).*

I love you Mummy.

Anita Ogbonna

5:45pm, 10*th* June

DECISIONS

Mummy,

    I am sorry I dozed past time. Did I leave you in suspense? I am sorry. Being an adult and all grown up is an interesting journey.

    I remember when I was about 7 years old and you asked what I wanted to be in the future. I can remember the surprise, yet hilarious and sarcastic look that you gave me when I said with confidence *"I want to be a grown up."*

    Instead of beating common sense into my head with cane like the eavesdropping neighbors had suggested, you took my arm and walked me to your room to tell me a story.

You said,

> *"It was a very cold evening, my father had just returned from his white collar job and my mother too had also just finished making dinner. I put a huge black kettle filled with water by the fire place to make the best of warm waters for my father to bathe. And then ran out to play a game. I was busy with my Nchorokoto; a game of four stones and 12 holes when I heard my mother call out from the kitchen "Ngooo leeh!!! Ma, I answered, "Ye zutalamihe oh!"*
>
> *"Come run some errands for me, she instructed. When I got to where she sent me, I could not*

find what she asked me to buy. Instead of buying the alternative products to what she asked me to buy I ran back home. My mother hit me so bad for my foolishness that day. When my dad got out of the showers and saw me crying, he asked "What happened?"

Amidst tears I explained the entire scenario and he started laughing. He laughed at this event so much that I asked angrily; "What is funny?" Then he said to me, as he pulled my head close to his waistline and smoothed my hair, "Your mother only wanted you to act as an adult and make a decision, using good discretion."

This story taught me that growing up is a matter of thoughts and actions, not mere words.

Anita Ogbonna

10:15am, 11th June

VAIN AND UNCERTAIN

Dear Mama,

Some guy tapped my shoulders. He looked really rough yet very friendly. He said that if I inhaled some of the burning grass he had on his palm, I would get over the feeling and then I could control myself even more.

Is this true mummy?

I am not even sure what this feeling he is selling is. I am scared but curious, and mummy it is drizzling here. I would smoke this to get warm and reduce the nauseating feeling that has erected sky scrapers in my body.

I prayed I didn't get addicted if it gave me succor. *(Took the first drag, choked, took the second drag).* It was not so bad after all (*I could use this to get warm and kill the images of the maggots in my head).*

When the rain was over, I got back on the bus. The routes were becoming more familiar and the effect of the smoke was kicking in. I thought I liked it as nothing had given me such comfort like this for a long time *(Admires her fingers nails).*

Vanity is still packed in her baggage.

Letters to Mama

6:15pm, 11th June

WET COALS AND EAST

The drizzles were getting heavier. I was stuck there with this rough looking guy and there was charcoal on the floor. That was the first time I would take a good look at where we had come to take refuge. It looked like a classroom. The dark walls had almost turned white.

I could see the beautiful art works made by spider's cobwebs on the almost dead roof. I guessed it was one of those places that I was familiar with. It wasn't his smoke that gave me that succor after all – it was the environment, a place of learning and growing.

(Strolled up casually to grab the piece of charcoal lying on the floor, only to find out it was wet). Wet coals don't make deep stains. I was going to get mad when the rough looking guy tapped my shoulder again.

As I looked up from where I was squatting, he pointed to the east and said, *"That's where the sun shines from."* I was about to ask what he meant when I heard the blare from the bus. Although I was running under the drizzles towards the bus I was doing this with so much excitement because I knew that when the rain ceased and I looked towards the east, the sun was bound to shine.

It seemed like new people are boarding our bus. I need to socialize.

3:14pm, 12th June

SOCIALIZE

Mummy!

I am glad I ran to the bus very quickly. I mingled with the new passengers.

The driver just announced that we are at our last bus stop so everyone would have to alight. I could have been alone by now if I had not spoken to anyone on the bus.

There is a lake behind the ocean, *(smiles)* and it is a beautiful one. The ocean always thought that the lake would run dry. I wonder why she forgets that she fuels the lake!

Letters to Mama

6:15pm, 12th June

POIGNANT AND RESTLESS

Mama,

      Did I tell you about the place where the oceans called home?

(*Takes in a deep breath tossed her pen up and down*).

Anita Ogbonna

03:45am, 13ᵗʰ June

COVERING SHAME

The gutter that I saw was a long narrow path. I think it ran into a canal, it had coverings that man could not see through properly, unless such a man strained his eyes.

(She paused like she wasn't certain, she wanted to tell her mother about her ordeal with the gutter but she hesitated then continued.)

One day, I woke up to find that the coverings of the gutter had been vandalized. There was a lot of baggage piled up in the gutter. Filth from all corners made their way into the gutter, so I, with the water from my ocean of kindness, decided to clean the ones nearer me.

Letters to Mama

11:00pm, 13th June

GOD'S MYSTERY

Mama,

I learnt that natural bodies of water have no definite shape. The oceans like, myself, settled and spread wherever it was welcomed.

I took the form of whatever life fills with me. I give life to the trees so that they can bear fruits for man to eat. You always said *"God is mysterious with many purposes"*.

I understand all that now mummy.

Anita Ogbonna

00:08pm, 14th June

UNSPOKEN WORDS AND PAIN

Dear Mama,

I... (*Tears filled her eyes and wet the almost empty page. She rumples the page and throws it at the extent of her rage.*)

Letters to Mama

8:59am, 15th June

A FRUITFUL END IS INNEVITABLE

Mother of a beautiful Ocean,

I have found a place I could lay my head, so that, even if it rained tonight, I won't be drenched. Even if the sun shines by day, my skin would not burn. But I do not know for how long I will stay here before the owners come to send me away.

I am sorry for keeping you in suspense for so long. Sometimes I wish I never started this journey but when I think of where I am heading to, I cringe with delight for the unknown.

12:13pm, 15th June

FRIENDSHIP

Mama,

I saw another Ocean, a powerful, strong, and mighty ocean. It roared but in peace and in serenity. It did not destroy and as it crossed paths with nature, it built, it gathered.

Our paths crossed.

We communicated and flowed into one another. Our connectivity became strong and as it said *"Let go!"*... I obeyed.

Letters to Mama

6:21 pm, 16th June

IN WEAKNESS, FIND STRENGTH AND BE STRENGTH!

Dear Mama,

I hope you are not worried. I know it is hard for every great mother to watch her little daughter go in search of food especially when she does not know where the source roosts. About this search, I am not totally proud of myself.

I went out as a lamb to a feast where lions and lionesses were both host and guest. I graced the lush field, ignorant of the pride's plot. They were gathered to prey, and I hoped you prayed harder than I do. I was a bait casted in the ocean with a hook to my mouth. There was a line, and there were sinkers, and immediately I touched the ocean, all the bigger animals came at me to glee or to feed. the smaller fishes were generous with pity, wishing they were this "I" but the bigger fins, came flapping at me, propelling eager mouths that bore jagged teeth, without liking for my survival. I was beyond scared, I was terrified. I couldn't swim, neither could I pull out from myself. I was trapped.

Do you know a man's tears are unknown in water; be it river or the ocean? Even with all the pains and the bruise in my soul, my tear drops were significant in the ocean that I am.

A *Psalm 23* is stuck on my lip.

Anita Ogbonna

00: 01am, 17ᵗʰ June

TREASURES

Dear Mama,
I know you still love jewels and precious stones.
I saw a lot of beautiful stones under the ocean of myself
And they don't even need to be processed.
They are in their natural form and their colors glow
I thought they would be much more appreciated
On the axis of the sun
They couldn't shine so much beneath the oceans
They needed the sun to shine
Mummy, you are my sun.

Beautiful Mama,
Thank you for birthing me.
Thank you for letting your golden ray
Reflect on the surface of the ocean
And penetrate the darkness at the bottom of the ocean

Letters to Mama

5:33pm, 17th June

TAKING CHANCES

Dear Mama,

I remember those days you told me that I shouldn't allow myself to be the victim and that I should defend myself whenever the need arose.

If I stayed calm, they would attack but if I put up a bold display to scare them off, before they noticed me, the sharks may still attack and either ways, I was done. Mummy, I will have to defend myself and take my chances.

I figured, from my lessons of discretion, that this is a nobler action – a clearer shot at survival!

Anita Ogbonna

6:59pm, 18th June

HOLDING UNTO DEATH FOR LIFE

Mama,

I remember another story in which you talked about your childhood. You said you went to fetch water with your peers. On getting to the stream, you all decided to have a quick bath. You filled your pot with water and quickly dived into the stream. The water was so refreshing, so much that you swam far to the other end. Out of sight, everyone thought you had drowned and they began to raise an alarm. Out of fear and realizing how far you had gone, you began to scream. You were drowning slowly.

You thought you could not swim back to the shore so you choose and begged God to console your parents if you drowned. When suddenly, your feet stepped on something like a spring and it pushed you above the water. You held unto a bamboo stick that was floating nearby and screamed out to your friends who had already called an older man working nearby the stream for help. He swam towards you and when he got to you, he asked that you climbed onto his back. When you got home that day, your mother, upon hearing the story, treated you like a newborn.

'How we hold onto death for life'

Maya Angelou – *"When it looked like the sun wasn't going to shine anymore, there was a rainbow in the clouds."*

Letters to Mama

11:32pm, 18th June

SELF APPRAISAL

Mummy,

I was still hungry but the pleasure and satisfaction that came with being out of the unsafe water would be food enough till I make it to the shore where I would have a decent meal.

The whales tossed me from one snout to another like I was their favorite play thing. I got scared of the heights at some time, but then I realized that they lacked the cruelty to toss me back to my ugly fate.

It felt like my mind held the reins of their motifs, so I steered us blissward.

Anita Ogbonna

11:32pm, 19th June

DEAR PILOT, TIME FLIES

Mummy,

     I was getting tired. I didn't even know where this path was leading us. It had been a really long journey. We walked unconsciously by daily events but when they become past, the desire to experience those events consciously kicked again. It was always too late.

     Sometimes, I wished that someone would take a stroll with me and show me these parts I have walked. I always looked forward, never really gathered all what happened within. I had struggled and survived these parts and now, I want to take all the risks. *(Jumps)*.

     Mummy, I see the people coming in different groups with different representatives. Lots of them.

Letters to Mama

10:01am, 20ᵗʰ June

STRONG

I have threaded a path that wasn't mine
But every time I had to pass
I had to be an ass.

I have been to shores
I have fought wars
And the falls, interesting sights
And swooshing sound that sends
Me a reminder that sometimes
Your fall is the slope
Giving the energy for your rise.

I'll keep fighting because
I know certain wars
Are inevitable and winners
Never quit on themselves.

Anita Ogbonna

11:13pm, 21ˢᵗ June

NAMES AND IDENTITY

(She begins to sing while she drums on her paper)

Nii muru nwa gere nu
Ndi muru nwa gere nu oh
Ndi muru nwa guo ya ezi aha, ihe aguru nwata
Ka ona abu
Oju nwoke na nwunye, muru nwa ha amaghi ihe ha gaa
kpo nwa ha
Ha guo ya obute
Obute toro wu nwoke ike, mana ebe obu na
Ogara oburu ihe ndi nma.
Obute toro ebe lebe egbuo

Parent Listen!
Parent Listen oh!!

He who has a child
should give him a befitting name
because what you call a child
is what he eventually becomes

Once, a man and a woman had a child
And they named him Obute, *(which means Carrier)*
Obute grew into a fine muscular young man
And his name manifested in his life well

Everywhere he went he carried and pilfered –
The hell in his name was let loose!

Letters to Mama

(I love to be called Grace)

Anita Ogbonna

8:14am, 22nd June

HEY MAMA

Dear Mama,

There are times when I get broken and I really missed you. *(Wipes the tear drops off her paper until the ink smudges on the paper).*

I love you Mummy.

Letters to Mama

9:42am, 23rd June

SOJOURN

Dear Mama,

      There are too many things that I would love to pen to you but my ink can't bear the burden of the heaviness in my heart any longer. Just like my pen, I have learnt that in our sojourn through life, our bodies and beauty may wear in the hands of age. But the quality we own, and our souls, will never fade.

00:24am, 24ᵗʰ July

NEVER DO MORE THAN YOU WILL BE APPRECIATED FOR

Dear Mama,

Do you remember a tale about death that you once told me? The narration went thus;

Death visited one of its victims and said to her, "Today, it's your turn, you shall join me on a journey on which you shall never return. But before we go, I need a glass of water." The woman went into her kitchen and prepared a feast for death and rather than the glass of water requested, she served death a glass of wine instead and the meal.

Death, out of deep satisfaction, fell asleep. So she seized the moment of his weakness to erase her name which was the first, on death's list and she wrote it at the last slot on the list.

When death woke up, he said to her; "You have been such a good host so I will do you a favor. Since I am inevitable on this earth, I will pass you by and choose my next victim from the bottom of my list. That way, you will have longer time to live on earth."

Death visited his next victim from the bottom of the list. Unfortunately, it was her. Death killed her.

Never cheat nature in its course, you will end up cheating yourself.

Never do more than you will be appreciated for. (I know better now)

1:27pm, 25th June

MAMA'S PRAYER

Mummy,

Please pray for me that all I have lost be nothing short of all I need to let go. That I may understand even the more, God's will for me. That the ocean is a tourist site for beauty and admiration, and more so, that it is a destructive ground.

Anita Ogbonna

3:16pm, 26th June

TO ALL THE WORDS THAT MY INK CAN'T TRACE OUT OF MYSELF

Letters to Mama

00:00am, 27th June

SELF DISCOVERY

Dear Mama,

 People ran towards the ocean, but where can the ocean run to? If water must always flow in the ocean, how do I truly find myself?

 I also searched for gold but I never found it. I never knew I was the gold. I kept pouring ink into the ocean and every time I poured in the ink, the oceans roared. Soon, the ink was all over my skin.

 Most of the ink went to my feet as the ocean hardly retains dirt on the surface. This could be likened to the moon that dies at dusk so that the sun can wear its crown at dawn.

 I, the ocean received renewal through whatever came my way, through dusk and dawn. I preserved the oceans' salt; the flavor man sought when ideal portion is served.

Anita Ogbonna

2:57pm, 28th June

VICTORY

I had my education
and a meager lush of innings.

I made deep marks on the limbo sides of life
and had my vast shares of tribulations
but a bigger courage to unwind
and pose history a bold question.

It was not long before I cast my die;
"if something never left your eyes
then there was a way about it".

Letters to Mama

5:46pm, 29th June

GRATITUDE

Dear Mama,

Thank you for teaching me
even when I never wanted to learn.
I learnt a lot
about the sword *'thank you', 'please',* and *'sorry'* wield

The ocean that begged for clean water often
But never knew that it is not the life that flows into her
that makes it salty,
Her tastiness and sassiness lives
within her soul and body.

Because I was the ocean,
The dark clouds that gathered over my head never bothered me.
I didn't even realize I was seated
under the dark patches of the pregnant sky.

My beautiful mother
Mama
Mother of the ocean, the sky has birthed its soul
And sees the beauty of its offspring within me.

It is raining and I am almost drowning
in over flowing happiness.
I begged for waters, he sent me showers
and he made me the ocean,

Anita Ogbonna

Let me create and be filled with salt because the world needs that flavor.

I am writing to you in a bit, this time I pray I share all the juicy details of procreation and motherhood.

Till then…

Letters to Mama

3:16pm, 26th June

THE END

To Mama
From your daughter
Grace

Anita Ogbonna

ABOUT THE AUTHOR

Anita Ogbonna is a creative writer born in the 90s. She aims to touch and encourage lives through written words in form of poetries and short stories. She is a prolific writer who believes in possibilities with the use of her literary imagination and reflective mindset.

ABOUT THE BOOK

Letters to Mama is a journey narrated by a young woman who leaves home at an early age. This book tells of her challenges and successes in the sequence of growing. Written in form of short letters and poems to her mother, she describes her transformation from a young woman to a strong and grown adult.

It is a book full of didactic meanings that awakens the hearts of young readers and guides them to make better decisions. It shows the hustles and challenges that she encounters during her sojourn. This book shows the effect of her decisions on her path through life.

In letter to mama, the author paints her imaginative path through figurative and metaphoric use of words. She describes people and events using natural bodies and non-living things.

Above all, the book; encourages better communication between parents and their children as it is also an ode to motherhood.